Copyright @ 2022 Christopher E. Singleton Sr.

To request permission, contact the author at

Write30haiku@gmail.com

Paperback: 978-1-7373779-9-3

Library of Congress Control Number:
2022905917

Cover Design by Dustin James

I Chris Singleton

With middle initial E

Wrote this haiku book

Do me a favor

If you like something I wrote

Share it & tag me

Write 30 Haiku In <30 Sunsets

Challenge Accepted

The First of Many

Message to the readers:

On February 22nd, 2021 I wanted to challenge myself by writing 30 haiku in 30 sunsets

I had so much fun writing, that I wrote over 30 haiku in less than 30 hours

I hope this book inspires you to write at least one

Intro to haiku

Here's a quick lesson

Haiku started in Japan

& was called hokku

It requires this

17 syllables max

No more & no less

Intro to haiku...continued

5 syllables here

This line 7 syllables

& this one has 5

I hope that was clear

Now, you know what to expect

It's time to begin

Family

Haiku for my mom

You had to deal with a lot

<u>Thanks</u> for everything

Family

To my wife, Toni

What can I do to <u>help</u> you?

To lighten your load

Being a dad

CJ Joshua

I promise to <u>love</u> you both

You light up my day

Being a dad

<u>Dad</u> life is awesome

Why do some ignore the call?

I just don't get it

Black History Month

Harriet Tubman

Thank you for your <u>sacrifice</u>

You are the real G·O·A·T·

Black History Month

Black History Month

You _deserve_ better than this

Maybe September?

Marvel

We know it is hard

Loving <u>someone</u> like Jean Grey

When she loves Cyclops

(Thanks Ivor)

Marvel

Many guessed it right

I can't wait to see what's <u>next</u>

On WandaVision

Desserts

Banana Pudding

The <u>best</u> dessert ever made

Sorry, not sorry

Desserts

Watergate salad

Brings back real good memories

Of my <u>grandmother</u>

There isn't a rewind button in life

Please take advantage

Of your <u>time</u> with family

A simple phone call

There isn't a rewind button in life

<u>Opportunities</u>

Deserve to be respected

For they are treasure

Writing

Sometimes we just need

To write that story with an

Unhappy <u>ending</u>

Writing

I am a writer

I do not fit in a <u>box</u>

But I prefer rhymes

"Acoustic Vibes" *

We heard great pieces

We heard talented artists

<u>Sundays</u> were awesome

"Acoustic Vibes" *

Had to do my part

So I created some dope

<u>Spotify</u> Playlists

Purpose

<u>What</u> is my purpose?

To be an inspiration

& love on people

Purpose

In Kindergarten

I knew I would be teaching

But <u>not</u> which age group

Back in the Day

Remember cassettes?

Waiting to record a song?

It taught us <u>patience</u>

Back in the Day

I <u>am</u> not Alvin

I am also not Simon

I am Theodore

Experience Blockers

Coronavirus

We had had enough of <u>you</u>

Time for you to go

Experience Blockers

I want to travel

But the <u>resources</u> aren't there

Thank you Sallie Mae

What I like

I like chocolate

Although, I don't like it <u>dark</u>

Give it to me white

What I like

Ultimate Frisbee

A very fun <u>game</u> to play

But it's exhausting

Reading

The dictionary

A long forgotten resource

A <u>wonderful</u> tool

Reading

Small way to help build

Your child's vocabulary

Simply, <u>read</u> to them

Untapped Potential

Wow, this is <u>crazy</u>

Who knew I could achieve this?

Hmm, I think God knew

Untapped Potential

Your gift can make room

If, you are nice to others

& support their <u>gift</u>

Social Media

To my dear <u>Clubhouse</u>

I can't do this every day

I still love you though

Social Media

Social media

You are a blessing to us

But also a curse

THE END, well kind of

The end of 30 haiku

But not of this book

To all the readers

Thank you for taking the time

To read my haiku

Now it is your turn

Find all the <u>underlined</u> words

& challenge yourself

Write 30 haiku

In less than 30 sunsets

Get ready, set, go!!!

How was I able to do this project?

I took a regular sheet of 8.5 x 11 printer paper and folded it four times...That's what you see on the front cover.

Since I was at work, I was able to pull it out, jot down a haiku as it came to mind, and put it back in my pocket... When I was finished, I typed it up, and came up with this...

If you have any questions about any of the haiku, feel free to reach out to me at

Write30haiku@gmail.com

Yes, I wrote a book

But you can write one as well

Or a few haiku

There is no pressure

To complete the task at hand

But... YOU CAN DO IT!!!

I hope what I wrote

Provides some inspiration

& encouragement

To get you to write

At least a haiku or two

Possibly 30

The * means

I had to edit the haiku

To make it make sense

Scan this QR code
To follow me on IG
& see some updates

Inspired? Then use

#write30haiku

& I will see yours

Bonus Haiku

Our black women
Have had to endure so much
Raising kids alone

Losing their children
To the streets and the police
Will it ever stop

When will the black men
Realize their influence
And step their game up

Teach boys to be men
To give respect to women
And to be fathers

Too many donors
Not enough dads in the world
Black men, let's change that

Queens, we are sorry
Sorry for the excuses
Sorry for the pride

We will be mentors
To our community
If you will have us

Bonus Haiku continued...

It is not too late
Your sons have mad potential
Your daughters do too

Let's work together
Let's get them on the right path
They will change the world

Cooperation
Will help heal our nation
Tell us what to do

We are listening
We want to be your shoulder
Not for you to cry

For you to relax
From all the work that you've done
And we were not there

We are ready now
Ready to be your support
Queens, we have your back

www.ingramcontent.com/pod-product-compliance
Lightning Source LLC
Chambersburg PA
CBHW042235090526
44589CB00001B/8